T0380886

Love Notes from God

Dear My Person . . .

BRITTANY SOUTHARD

Interior Art Credit: Brittany Southard

WestBow Press books may be ordered through booksellers or by contacting:

WestBow Press
A Division of Thomas Nelson & Zondervan
1663 Liberty Drive
Bloomington, IN 47403
www.westbowpress.com
1 (866) 928-1240

ISBN: 978-1-9736-1827-0 (sc)
ISBN: 978-1-9736-1828-7 (e)

Library of Congress Control Number: 2018901371

Print information available on the last page.

WestBow Press rev. date: 7/23/2018

WESTBOW
PRESS®
A DIVISION OF THOMAS NELSON
& ZONDERVAN

First and foremost, I dedicate this collection of awesome findings to my first love, the lover of my soul, my Abba Father. Your never-ending compassion causes my spirit to pause daily. What intimate details Your love notes chiseled into my being, so that I might share Your mercy with, so many lonely hearts. The most important legacy a parent can leave a child, is that of a firm foundation in Jesus Christ. Dad…mom… I cannot thank you enough for the values you taught your children and for the love and encouragement you give so freely to all of us. Just merely saying "I love you" is such an understatement.

What would a book dedication be if you didn't share the sunshine that inspired you to see this whole experience through. My Auntie Ina, your contagious laughter and your joy that shines so brightly in the midst of any circumstance has been a light to my soul. I thank you for those six little words from your heart, "you need to write a book." I love you and adore you.

Hunter Southard, my sweet nephew, my purest sense of joy. Watching you grow has been the most complete and inspirational blessing in my life. Your innocence and blind faith in Jesus has made this journey so easy. You are my muse. You are everything good. I love you more than words can say.

I call this my season of being still, my season in waiting, and at times, my season of loneliness. Let's get really real. Holidays, celebrations, church get-togethers, they can be the best, but when you look down that church pew at couple after couple, or watch people in duos laughing over spaghetti in a restaurant, or you're that odd ticket at the movies surrounded by a bunch of even ticket goers, it can sting. It makes you ask that question… a lot. "Amazing God, the power who hung the stars, where in this world is my pew sitting, ticket holding, couples dining only, soulmate? I found myself not disrespecting the Almighty of Everything, but my questions just seemed to purely and innocently flow. "God, Master Potter, I know that he's been created just for me. I know that the minute You fashioned me and placed me in my mother's womb You knew my hearts desires, so You had to create my significant other, right? So, where is he? Did he get lost? They say I have a ticking clock, a time table I need to keep up with, and I am… just to be honest… anxious. As satan does… he would so unexpectedly plant those seeds of doubt and despair… an invitation to a wedding of a darling twenty-year young couple… a well-meaning friend asking me if I was married… endless baby showers of those much younger than myself… I couldn't help but wonder, "what in the world am I doing wrong?" I'm trying to do all things pure, all things according to the Word, all thoughts and actions taken captive for such a time as this, I'm still very single. I'm still very alone at the Valentine's day banquet, still struggling with the concept that something is wrong with me. The truth is you can only have so many conversations and hear so many versions of how your life will, or should play out, before you start to make notes for yourself. Let's see… should I try a dating site and help God out? He's so busy, maybe this one issue has just temporarily slipped His all-knowing magnificent mind? You begin to review your qualifications for that perfect man as if God doesn't work in the area of perfect details. "Okay… maybe we can leave off the blue eyed, dark hair thing so as not to weaken the pot?" Scratching details off my list just became confusing. So many opinions and so little time… "Oh girl, you just might as well become a nun. "You are looking for something that does not exist!" So I would consider that wise advice and scratch off "needs to play the guitar." With each little check mark came a great sense of loss. I was doubting the ability of the Creator of the Universe. The very one that created "all" in six days. The God so dedicated to detail that we have a hard time coming up with names for the different colors of green. During each attempt someone would make to "help" God along, He still remained utterly faithful. He would send me across the paths of just the right encouragers, a grounded preacher that would insist I increase my list's demands. This man of God so graciously share that God had given him his perfect person right down to the butterfly tattoo. Most would seem aghast that I was asking for a virtuous man at thirty years old, but God in His faithfulness would direct my mind to an article on social media. A story all about a 30 something, Christian man who was choosing to wait, or a married couple that had remained pure until they said those so important, yet so simple words, "I do." With each act of mercy and compassion, I began to know Him in such an intimate way. God had my backside. My father had my future, and He didn't need any help. I began to add to my already long list… "He needs to love my nephew like his own… I'm definitely keeping the dark hair and blue eyes! "He needs to love Missouri, and I'm not scratching that guitar playing ability he is going to have to have, off the list "Jesus was a carpenter, so I'm sure that I'm not asking too much with the request that he be handy with a hammer and nails. With each new insight God showed me, my faith would soar, and my appetite for all He could be to me in this waiting period became insatiable. I asked him to show me more. I wanted to walk faithfully, without hesitation, into his ideal plan for my life. I was so grateful for His continuous encouragement through so many doubts, and I just wanted to know He had my hearts desires still steadfast on His mind. That simple prayer… that blind faith… It threw open the door to me finding "love" everywhere… in all things… all over the place. Sometimes in the most simple, and silly things, and always it would direct me to a place of assurance and peace. He had this, and "this" was good. You know, you just do not want to get ahead of God.

You know, you just do not want to get ahead of God.

When a gal has six brothers, she is given a front row seat to the world of dating. I've basically learned what not to do. Watching the struggles of so many relationships led me to one conclusion, I didn't want to experience that type of heartbreak. The dating game always led to someone's brokenness. I begin to see "dating" as a bad way to a good thing. God had to have a better plan… a perfect timing. As I examined my heart deeply in this area, I began to grow closer to my Lord. A new trust and commitment to His perfect will began to well up inside me, and I had a deep need to know my God even deeper. My Lord quickly revealed that marriage minded people squander precious time in this dating minded world. I've seen relationships go on for years, both knowing that if they were meant to marry it would have happened long before now. I've watched these 'relationships' drain the life out of people. I've watched individuals that gave too much too soon, leave with parts of their hearts out there forever. They struggle to move on just to repeat the same lonely scenarios. I started to see a real beauty in waiting on God. I knew this wait could be lonely and uncertain, that is when I decided to fleece God. I didn't want to make a mistake. I couldn't afford to guess. This is when the 'list' came to life. A small piece of paper, a covenant between me and my God. This list would leave no doubt, no uncertainty. Talk about free falling, the ultimate trying of faith. I knew that friends and family would not just find me peculiar, but some might call me downright strange. Not only did my prayers become quite specific, my future had a list. I know, I know…God didn't need it in writing, but that was my outward commitment of extreme faith and it made me feel better. He showed me that His standards are even higher than mine. He taught me just how little of a tail I was, and that I was not only the head of this serpent, but a princess and that I should act like one. In this complete surrender and enlightenment, I found such excitement in God's complete ability to write my love story.

I quickly learned that although my faith was strong and my soul at peace, it wasn't quite the same with others. I call them wet blankets… dream catchers, and God helpers. A wet blanket will not hesitate in sharing their opinion quickly and without remorse. "Girl, you are never getting married! Giving God a list like that may be going against His perfect will. What if He put blonde hair on the man He made for you?! You are limiting God!" They can leave the deepest faith shaking in it's boots. I would find in those times, that I would lift my eyes towards heaven just ever so slightly, as not to waver, but there was just a second of doubt, "did you get that God?" These discouragers are probably the ones that leave you most hopeless. They seem to know their stuff and the Bible. They don't mess around and they usually walk off shaking their heads confidently, as if they have just imparted wisdom to you and changed your whole thought process with three sentences. They usually leave the room with a "you just think about what I'm saying to you…" The problem is, if you don't start praying and pressing in, you will.

Then there are the dream catchers, those folks will ride with you for a while. They start out thinking that your list is amazing and they can see great potential in this type of complete faith. They like the idea of fleecing God and holding firm. They pretty much line up with every part of your spirit until you hear that first "but?" That dreaded word, you know it is coming and it won't be pretty… "what if God does not intend that you marry?" "What if God wants you in missions to orphans, and you are praying to bring more children into this world?" "What if these are your desires, and not God's." Yes… that dream catcher snatches that hope right out of your hands, and temporarily holds it ransom. You see that little cottage and baby powder smell hanging somewhere in between nowhere, and no way. As if someone just put a wall up that you must navigate some strategic plan to get around. Let's not forget that God can plant the desires of His heart into your heart pretty easily. I've heard stories of children, as young as five, being called into missions. I can usually recover from a well-meaning dream catcher more easily. I rationalize with great speed, that the Almighty God who controls the universe, can quickly change the desire my heart holds now, if His intentions are not my own. I feel like superwomen at that point and I punt kick that wall down immediately. I can walk away pretty confident from a dream catcher. They usually leaved more confused than I ever was. I become the encourager. I find myself sharing just how powerful and all-knowing my God is, and that He will change my heart's desire… and if not… I'll just stay on this path with a tight grip clinching my list.

God helpers are probably my favorite. They will usually line up with not one thing I believe. They are the ones that have a friend of a cousin in mind. They are lovers of dating sites and small get togethers. They are transparent, non-critical and easy keepers. They always resort back to one plan. It usually involves strangers that hold possible potential. They will take your list and check it twice. You will show up to a party that is composed of two married women and five brown haired, blue eyed men, all of them learning to play guitar. Imagine the shock when you find a wonderful profile describing the princess you are on five Christian dating sites and every married woman brings their third cousin to church on social Sundays. These people entertain you. They have more ideas and theories than Einstein. If it wasn't the fact that I find all that a little frightening, they might be able to sneak in my backdoor without me noticing. They never hurt my feelings or leave me hopeless. I like their methods the best. They usually will change the subject when they see you aren't grabbing hold, and that's just fine with them. You exasperated them, and it wears out their brain. I usually have a moment of snickering with God, and inform Him that He better drop that dating app thing in my mailbox like an elephant into a rabbit hole, if that is His method.

So… what am I really saying is I consciously choose on a daily basis not to let negativity leave me hopeless, desperate, or afraid. I capture my peace with every thought. No joy stealers aloud. Go ahead, make me laugh. I need all that God given medicine I can get. I occupy my heart and mind with a perfect God who holds the perfect will for my life as a top priority, because I trust in Him. My King is cheering me on and working behind the scenes. It is well with my soul on all accounts. I so anticipate the day that My God brings great testimony to so many. I expect above all things, that God will use all He is staging to show His great and powerful capabilities to so many. I pray He is magnified through this journey, and that He shows off in big ways. I pray my testimony and walk will encourage others to stay the path, trust completely, and hold on to hope through Jesus Christ. He is that blanket of warmth and comfort, the ultimate dream maker and He needs absolutely no help in bringing His will full on. So, I'm setting quietly knowing who I believe in, and He graciously given my soul revival in knowing how this pleases Him.

I know, you want hard facts on how I really get through those lonely or awkward moments. You want to know if I cry at all on Valentine's day? You have this need to understand how in the world do you just sit and wait for your miracle. Easy… I don't carry a burden that is not mine to bare. I put this request in the perfect place a long time ago. Now my heart chooses Him. I seek Him in all things. I'm a lover of His creation. Nothing is more peaceful than conversing with God. One gorgeous day, while sipping tea on the front porch, I asked God to give me a glimpse into His desire for my life. What is truly my calling? Will I have my own person to share life with? I always wait on His answers, try not to speculate, or get in a hurry. He is faithful to talk back to me, even if it is weeks later. This day was one of those jump up and down days. He answered so quickly, and in such a way He knew I would notice. This big blue butterfly fluttered by me so close that I thought it would land on my nose. The reason it didn't…another big blue butterfly was just inches behind the first. They looked like the merry-go-round of butterflies, one up and one down, but never further than an inch apart. He spoke to my spirit man. It was a pair. A direct answer to a specific question.

Oh, how good and faithful my listening and caring God is. He could have not answered. It could have been just one. I knew in this moment that I wanted Him to talk to me specifically every day, out loud and personally. I needed a tangible presence of an intangible God. So, I asked…" talk to me Lord, make your presence known to me on a daily basis. Show me every day just how much you love me. Although I know all these things, my heart delights in your Presence, and my soul sings when you speak to me. God opened a new season in my life and used His glorious masterpiece to minister to me throughout each and every day. I fell in love with His creation. I started to notice how many different birds there were, how there was color inside of color, and the sounds were nothing but that of praise by all that He had made. Each season brought it's own beauty and transparency of how God intended it to work. I discovered first hand His truth in what He meant when He said that no man could find any excuse to not believe in Him when looking at all He crafted. I began to walk with Him, talk with Him, explore thought with Him. I sang praises to Him as the crickets and birds did, and I was so glad they were there for backup. I am pretty sure that a worship leader is not in my future. I'm just as sure that those awkward melodies went straight to the ears of God, and it made Him smile. Then it happened…that amazing day…there on my hotdog was a heart from His heart. He drew my attention to this perfect mustard and ketchup transformation, A tiny heart, all yellow and red, and shinning so brightly. It was all I could see. That great day, it just happened, my first love note from God. I knew I needed to get a photo of what just was implanted into my soul forever. "He's talking to me?! "The God of the universe is conversing with me!" From that day on… hearts in everything, everywhere, and as I shared so many others were ministered to by Him. Some days there were many, and some days only one, but whatever each day brought, it was a perfect reminder that He was with me, and loved me, and had me. I began to look forward to getting up. It was like Christmas morning. I couldn't wait to see what I would find. They were all so differently molded, or sculpted or the perfect accident allowed for that perfect shape. Each one told me just how pleased my God was. I could hear Him so profoundly. "My dear little girl, dear daughter of mine, you have made me your first love, and you are precious in my sight." You have sought Me above all things. I will give so many perfect gifts to you in this life. "I have great plans for you"." I will never leave you". "You are never alone"" I will prosper you, and yours, and protect you from harm". "As we journey through this season, I will magnify my glory through you". "As you share this time with others, many will trust and believe in a perfect love, because you will have shown them the heart of God". And not the heart of man. To everything there is a season, and through this season, I not only walk with you, I will create a ministry within your heart. "I will be reminding you of great rewards." "that await" …Never stop in your search to know my heart." Sitting so silently in that moment, I knew one thing…another love note was on its way!

Dear My Person...
Yum! Ketchup, and mustard...
a little twang with my sugar!

Dear My Person...

I Love to watch poodles turn into hippos,

and hippos turn into ice cream cones...and then just fade away....

Dear my person...
I don't like spiders or snakes,
but a little green frog with a heart on it...
a kiss away from a prince!

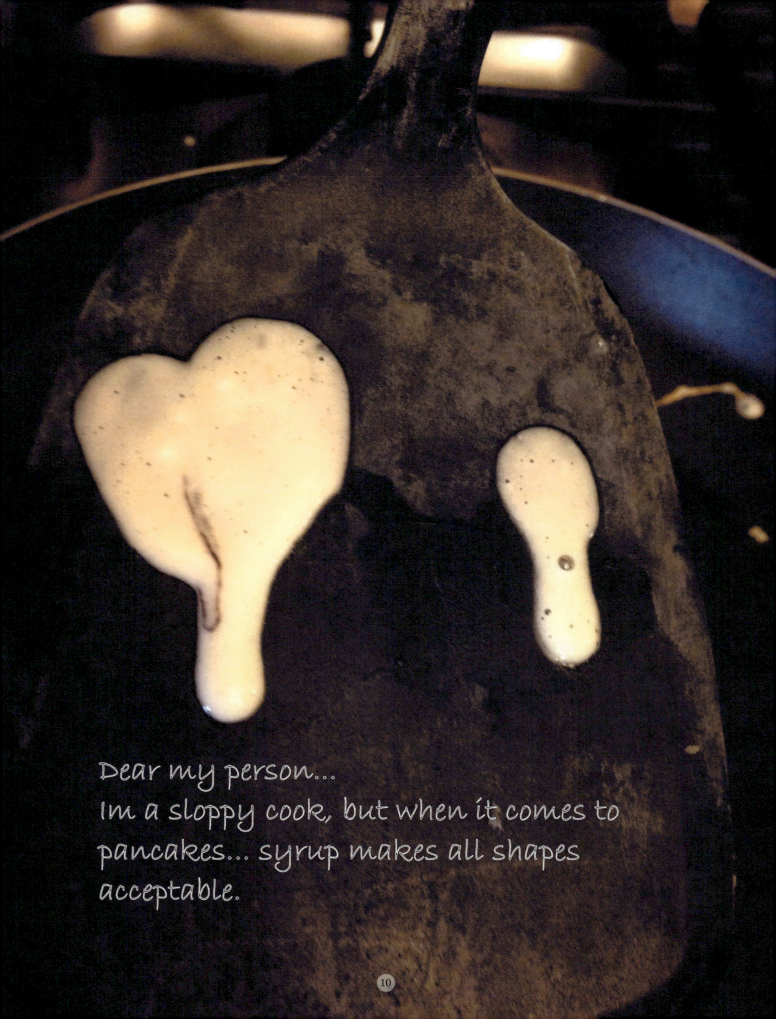

Dear my person...
Im a sloppy cook, but when it comes to
pancakes... syrup makes all shapes
acceptable.

Dear My Person..
grilled,fried,sliced...
everything but your breath
is better with an onion!

Dear my person...
some of the greatest art pieces
I discovered hiking with my
Jesus.

Dear my person...
Better than the toy!! A heart shaped nugget!

Dear my person...
I'm not a big fruit person, but who can resist a
juicy red cherry...with a heart inside

14

Dear my person...
anything having to do with a
banana should be attached with bread...

Dear my person…
the only thing I liked about this icing
was its color. and the little pink heart stain from
the way too rich grease.

Dear my person...
Im hopelessly loyal.
You can chisel that
in a rock.

Dear my person...
I love orange juice...

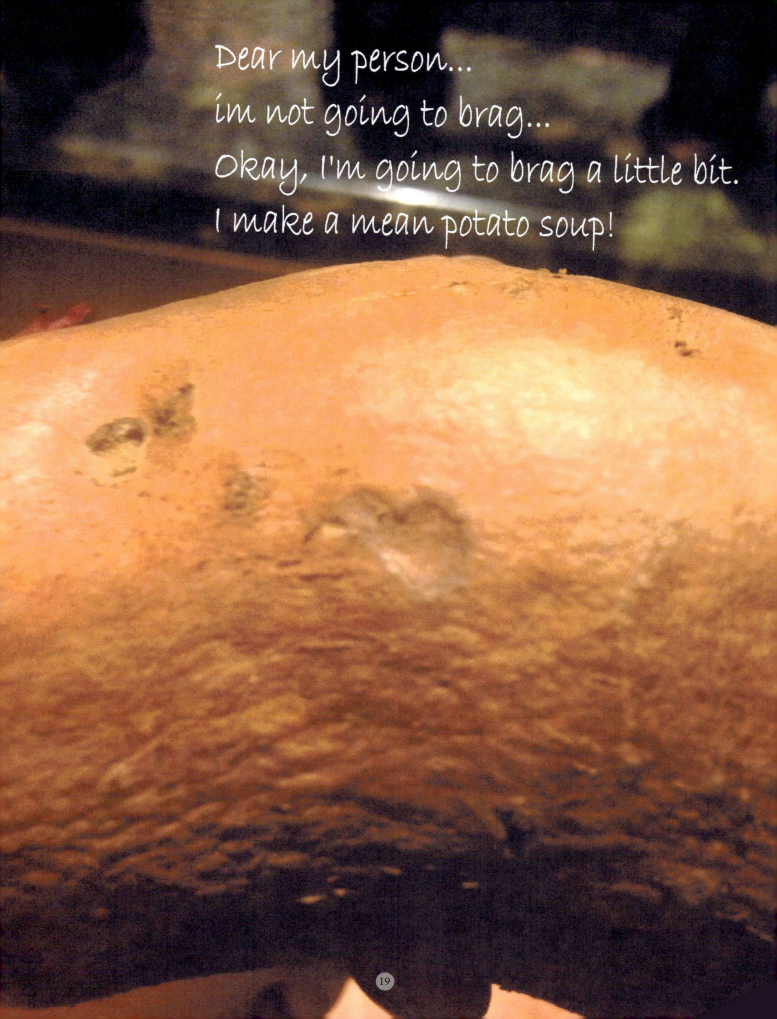

Dear my person...
im not going to brag...
Okay, I'm going to brag a little bit.
I make a mean potato soup!

Dear my person...
no double dipping!

Unique Mexican
Bar & Grill
573-336-4373

ters & Nachos

Nachos Juss

Cheese nachos topped with cha
beans. Covered with chee
es and sour cream 7.95

p Cocktail
shrimp topped with sp
slices of avocado

Nachos Espe
ked with zucchi
tomatoes and mu
dip 10.99

mp Nachos
d of crispy tortilla chip
rimp, onions, tomato
dip 12.99

Chicken Wings
Our chicken wings de
special sauce 7.99

Brav
hos w
ked with
red with

Guacamo
fectly ripened avoc   with
ns, cilantro, jalapenos   fresh

Cheese Nachos 4
Cheese and Jalap
Beef Nachos 6.9
Beef and Bean
Chicken Nacho

Dear my person...
I love lighting...mood lighting...
Christmas lights....candle light...
stars...sigh

Dear my person...
Ice cream without chocolate
is milk...unless you throw
in some peppermint...

22

Dear my person...
Blue skies for me.
gray skies...seriously challenged!

Dear my person..
My favorite...sweet and sour
chicken. My taste buds preefer
polar opposites. Lemon in sweet tea,
chocolate on pretzels, honey and
mustard...and on and on

Dear my person...
I should have picked this up and put four steel legs
on it... an industrial looking end table with a
heart...now thats beautiful!

Dear my person...
In a world where everyone wants to be
a star, be a heart.

Dear my person...
I love my vegetables,
but I prefer them in ranch dip.

Dear my person...
I love just a little bit of syrup..
Wink..wink.

Dear my person...
Do you believe in the cookie monster?
I've met her...

Dear my person...
I like a little enchilada
with my sour cream...a
little potato with my
sour cream...a little sour
cream with my sour
cream...

Dear my person...
I like things clean, shinning, and bright.
I inspect all forks in a restaurant.

Dear my person...
there was a little salad on my salad.
if only it would have been cotton candy.

Dear my person...
one gals trash is another gals treasure.

Dear my person...
a pair of rain boots, and nothing
stomps me!

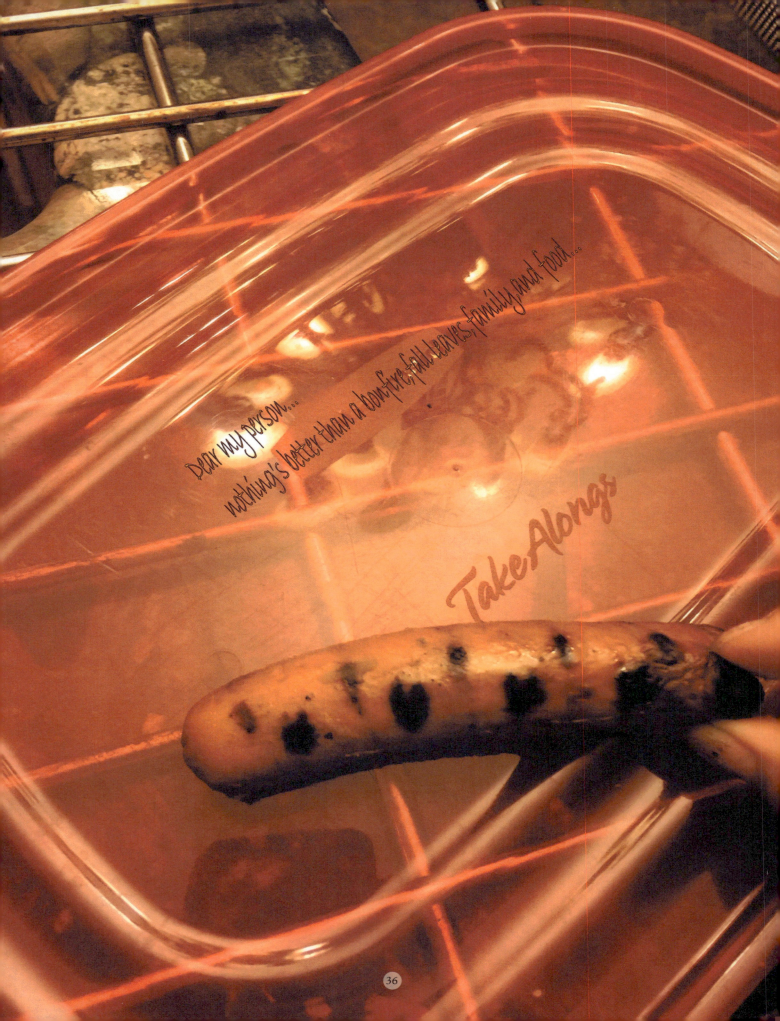

Dear my person...

nothing's better than a bonfire, fall leaves, family and food...

Take Alongs

Dear my person...
it's all about the little imperfect
pieces coming together to make a rock
solid foundation.

Dear my person...
Im a hopeless romantic,
nothing like a heart on a red rose
to say I love you...Thank you Jesus.

Dear my person...
nothing like a sea shell to show
the fine art skills of a master creator...
one you cannot deny...

Dear my person...
coffee...
Gods gift to mornings.

40

Dear my person...
His principles are
carved deep into
my soul. They
will endure with
me forever.

Dear my person...
I love the ocean...
when water sparkles
like diamonds...

42

Dear my person...
Chocolate...enough said.

Dear my person...
Equally yoked
Gods perfect plan.

Dear my person…
Single is just a word.
I grow everyday, as he
reveals himself to me.
Jesus is my true vine
I pray always to bear good fruit.

Dear my person...
A smile says so much
about the soul...
Smile with your whole
face!

Salvation Plan

Prayer

SALVATION PRAYER

Dear God in heaven, I come to you in the name of Jesus.

I acknowledge to You that I am a sinner, and I am sorry for my sins and the life that I have lived; I need your forgiveness.

Right now I confess Jesus as the Lord of my soul. With my heart, I believe that God raised Jesus from the dead. This very moment I accept Jesus Christ as my own personal Savior and according to His Word, right now I am saved.

Thank you Jesus for your unlimited grace which has saved me from my sins. I thank you Jesus that your grace never leads to license, but rather it always leads to repentance. Therefore Lord Jesus transform my life so that I may bring glory and honor to you alone and not to myself.

Thank you Jesus for dying for me and giving me eternal life. AMEN